Bryce Harper

By Jon M. Fishman

AMAZING ATHLETES

⌐ Lerner Publications Company • Minneapolis

Lerner Publications Company
A division of Lerner Publishing Group, Inc.
241 First Avenue North
Minneapolis, MN 55401 USA

For reading levels and more information, look up this title at www.lernerbooks.com.

Library of Congress Cataloging-in-Publication Data

Fishman, Jon M.
    Bryce Harper / by Jon M. Fishman.
        pages   cm. — (Amazing athletes)
    Includes index.
    ISBN: 978–1–4677–2143–1 (lib. bdg. : alk. paper)
    ISBN: 978–1–4677–2438–8 (eBook)
    1. Harper, Bryce, 1992—Juvenile literature. 2. Baseball players—United States—Biography—Juvenile literature. I. Title.
GV865.H268F57 2014
796.357092—dc23 [B]   2013037650

Manufactured in the United States of America
1 – BP – 12/31/13

TABLE OF CONTENTS

Bryce Harper is one of the most powerful hitters in baseball.

SHOW OF POWER

Washington Nationals **outfielder** Bryce Harper swung with all his might. *Crack!* The ball sailed through the night sky. It cleared the outfield wall for a **home run**. Bryce would hit many more home runs that night.

Bryce was swinging in the 2013 **Home Run Derby**. The derby takes place the day before the **Major League Baseball (MLB) All-Star Game**. Bryce was only 20 years old at the time. It was an honor for someone so young to be in the Home Run Derby. The event was also special for Bryce because his dad pitched to him.

Bryce's father, Ron Harper, pitches to his son.

Bryce watches the ball soar through the sky.

When Bryce was a kid, his dad often threw batting practice for his son. "I'd just swing and try to hit the ball as hard as I could," Bryce said. At the age of 10, Bryce told his dad that if he ever made it to the Home Run Derby, he wanted his dad to pitch to him. That's exactly what happened 10 years later. "It's a dream come true," said Ron Harper.

The young star hit eight homers in the first round. In the second round, he hit the ball over the fence on five straight swings. He finished the round with another eight home runs. Bryce had slugged his way to the final round.

Bryce had fun at the All-Star Game. "Being able to play with the best players in baseball is always a blast," he said. "I'm looking forward to a couple more All-Star Games."

Yoenis Cespedes of the Oakland A's was the other player in the final round. Bryce switched to a lighter bat. Swinging so many times had tired him out. He still managed to put eight more balls into the seats for home runs. But it wasn't enough. Cespedes hit nine homers to win the derby.

Bryce's father *(right)* was proud to pitch to his son at the Home Run Derby.

Bryce always wants to win. But he was happy to have given his best effort alongside his dad. "I always hit well off my dad," Bryce said. "I'm so thankful and blessed he was able to do that."

Bryce was raised in the city of Las Vegas, Nevada.

PRACTICE, PRACTICE, PRACTICE

Bryce Aron Max Harper was born in Las Vegas, Nevada, on October 16, 1992. His parents are Ron and Sheri. His older brother's name is Bryan. Ron is an ironworker. He helps construct new buildings. Sheri works in a law office.

Like this young slugger, Bryce played T-ball at an early age.

Baseball has always been important to the Harper family. Ron often took his sons to local parks after work. They went through batting and fielding **drills**.

Bryce played on a T-ball team before he was old enough for school. He was better at the sport than other players his age. His parents moved him up to play against older kids. Bryce would often compete against older players as the years went on.

Bryce got better and better as he grew. By the time he was 10 years old, he was playing on **travel teams**. Some of the teams were from other states. Bryce played as many as 130 baseball games each year. He became well known among youth baseball players and coaches.

At the age of 12, Bryce played for the McDowell Mountain Yankees. The team's home field is in Scottsdale, Arizona. They traveled to play in **tournaments** all around the country. Former Yankees coach Brad Tingley remembers a trip to New York with Bryce. "Everybody knew Bryce then," Coach Tingley said. "I remember people running around trying to get his autograph the day we checked in."

Baseball has always been Bryce's favorite sport. But when he was in school, he also played football and liked to snowboard.

People who saw Bryce play were impressed. Some of them even began talking about the young player making it to the major leagues someday. But Bryce wasn't ready to look that far ahead. "I wasn't really thinking about that at that age," Bryce said. "You just think about playing ball and going home after the game and swimming."

Bryce was larger than most other kids his age in high school.

HEAD OF THE CLASS

Bryce entered Las Vegas High School as a freshman in 2007. He was growing fast. At only 15 years old, he could hit the ball farther than anyone in his school. Bryce bashed a huge home run in a game in the spring of 2008. His coaches later went out to the field to measure the distance of the hit. It was 570 feet. This is an incredible distance for a home run to travel.

By his sophomore season, Bryce towered over most of his schoolmates. He was six feet three inches tall. He weighed more than 200 pounds. He mostly played **catcher** on his high school team. He also pitched. **Scouts** clocked some of his throws at 96 miles per hour.

Bryce often played catcher on his high school team.

Bryce poses in his 16U National Team uniform.

After the high school season, Bryce played on USA Baseball's 16U National Team. This team is for top players aged 16 years old or younger. They traveled to Mexico for the Pan Am Championships.

Bryce had a fantastic tournament in Mexico. His **batting average** was .571. He crushed four home runs and ran for six **stolen bases**. He also pitched the final inning of a 3–1 win over Cuba. Bryce was named the team's Most Valuable Player (MVP).

Baseball scouts around the country were convinced that Bryce could be a great MLB player someday. The young slugger agreed. Becoming a professional baseball player as soon as possible became Bryce's number one goal.

Bryce's parents were also sure that their son could be a star someday. To help Bryce reach his dream, Ron and Sheri made a decision that many people disagreed with. They allowed their son to drop out of high school after just two years.

By dropping out of high school, Bryce could attend classes at the nearby College of Southern Nevada (CSN). He would learn a lot from the older players at CSN. Leaving high school after the spring of 2009 would also allow Bryce to enter the 2010 MLB **draft**.

Bryce holds up the US flag during his time on the 16U National Team.

Bryce worked hard to make it on the CSN baseball team.

MOVING UP

Bryce had work to do before he could play on the CSN baseball team. He needed to pass the General Educational Development (GED) tests. He did so in December 2009. By passing the GED tests, Bryce showed that he had learned about as much as students who had completed high school.

Bryce's first games with CSN came on a weekend at the end of January 2010. About 1,400 fans showed up at the stadium each day. These were the biggest crowds in CSN baseball history. As many as 100 scouts also went to the games to see Bryce. In the third game of the weekend, he hit his first college home run.

Bryce runs to first base after hitting the ball.

Bryce often played catcher for CSN.

The CSN coaches were happy with Bryce. The scouts were too. They knew that college baseball was a tough test for such a young player. "He's a 17-year-old kid playing against older kids that are out to get him," a scout said.

After hitting his first home run, Bryce went on a hot streak that lasted the rest of the year. When the season ended, he led his team in a bunch of statistics. He was tops in batting average (.443) and home runs (31). He also had the most **runs batted in (RBIs)** and runs scored with 98 of each.

Most college baseball players stay at their schools for a few years. But Bryce had made it clear that he planned to enter the 2010 MLB draft. He could return to CSN if he couldn't work out a **contract** with the MLB team that chose him.

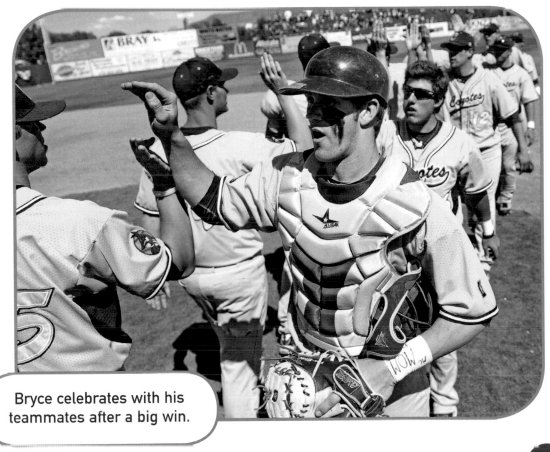

Bryce celebrates with his teammates after a big win.

On June 7, 2010, the Nationals chose Bryce with the first pick in the draft. The team announced right away that they would move their new star to the outfield. Bryce would miss playing catcher. But he was willing to do what his new team thought best. "Anywhere they need me, I'll play," he said.

The Nationals also had the first pick in the 2009 MLB draft. They chose pitcher Stephen Strasburg.

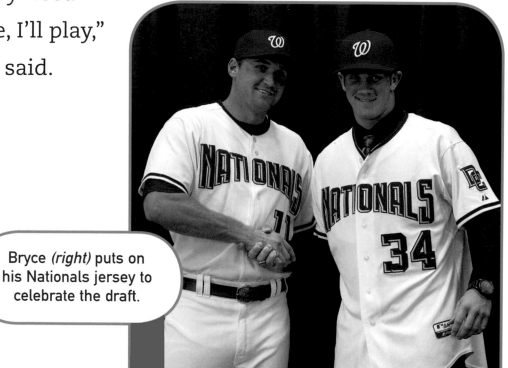

Bryce *(right)* puts on his Nationals jersey to celebrate the draft.

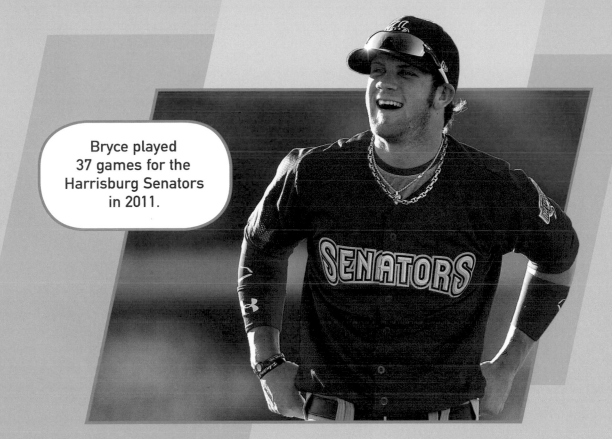

Bryce played 37 games for the Harrisburg Senators in 2011.

YOUNGEST ALL-STAR

Before Bryce could join the Nationals, he and the team had to agree to a contract. Over two months, the two sides worked out their differences. Bryce finally signed his contract on August 17. Washington agreed to pay him $9.9 million over five years.

Bryce warms up before batting during a minor-league game.

Like most players, Bryce began his professional career in the **minor leagues**. He smacked 17 home runs in 109 games with two minor-league teams in 2011. But in 2012, Bryce would play only 21 games in the minors.

The Nationals called Bryce up on April 27, 2012. Washington had planned to leave Bryce in the minor leagues for a while longer. But the team needed him to replace an injured player. Bryce was still just 19 years old. That made him the youngest Nationals player ever.

Bryce gets ready to swing while playing for the Nationals.

Bryce shows off his skills on the field.

Bryce played his first game with the Nationals in Los Angeles. They faced the Dodgers. The rookie stayed calm before the game, but he knew that feeling wouldn't last. "Once the lights turn on and the fans get here, that's when my energy level is going to jump through the roof," he said. Bryce hit a **double** in the game for his first MLB hit.

The Nationals' new star stayed in the majors for the rest of the season. In July, he replaced an injured player on the 2012

National League (NL) All-Star team. This made Bryce the youngest position player to make the All-Star Game in history. A position player is any baseball player who is not a pitcher. In 2013, fans voted Bryce to the All-Star Game. He became the youngest position player to ever start an All-Star Game the day after almost winning the Home Run Derby.

Bryce *(center)* runs the bases at the 2012 MLB All-Star game.

In fewer than two full MLB seasons, Bryce has already launched more than 40 home runs. Many people think he has what it takes to become the best player in the game. "Bryce has a saying," said his dad. "Whenever people say how good he is, he likes to say 'I'm not done yet. I still have work to do.' He's going to get a lot better."

Bryce was named the 2012 NL Rookie of the Year.

Bryce prepares to make a catch.

Selected Career Highlights

2013 Became the youngest position player to start in an All-Star Game

2012 Called up to the Nationals
Hit 22 home runs in 139 games with the Nationals
Became the youngest position player to play in an All-Star Game
Named National League Rookie of the Year

2011 Hit 17 home runs with a .297 batting average in the minor leagues

2010 Chosen with the first pick in the MLB draft
Signed a $9.9 million contract with Washington
Led College of Southern Nevada in home runs, RBIs, batting
average, and runs scored

2009 Left high school after two years
Named MVP of USA Baseball's
16U National Team after the
Pan Am Championships

2008 Hit a 570-foot home run as a
high school freshman

Glossary

All-Star Game: a game played in the middle of each MLB season, featuring the top players of the American League and the National League

batting average: a number that describes how often a baseball player gets a hit

catcher: the player behind home plate who catches throws from the pitcher

contract: a deal agreed to and signed by a player and a team. A contract includes the amount of money the player will earn and the number of years the player will play.

double: a hit that allows a batter to reach second base

draft: a yearly event in which teams select high school and college players

drills: exercises done to learn skills

home run: a hit that allows a batter to run all the way around the bases to score a run

Home Run Derby: a yearly event in which baseball players take turns batting to see who can hit the most home runs

Major League Baseball (MLB): the top level of professional baseball in the United States and Canada

minor leagues: a series of teams in which players gain experience and improve their skills before going to the major leagues

National League (NL): one of MLB's two leagues. The NL has 15 teams, including the Washington Nationals, New York Mets, Los Angeles Dodgers, and others.

outfielder: a person who plays in the outfield

runs batted in (RBIs): the number of runners able to score on a batter's hit or walk

scouts: people who judge the skills of a player

stolen bases: moves from one base to the next while the pitcher is throwing the ball to home plate

tournaments: events in which teams compete to decide a champion

travel teams: teams of young players that travel long distances to play games

Further Reading & Websites

Fishman, Jon M. *Mike Trout*. Minneapolis: Lerner Publications, 2014.

Kennedy, Mike, and Mark Stewart. *Long Ball: The Legend and Lore of the Home Run*. Minneapolis: Millbrook Press, 2006.

Savage, Jeff. *Stephen Strasburg*. Minneapolis: Lerner Publications, 2013.

The Official Site of Major League Baseball
http://www.mlb.com/home
Major League Baseball's official website provides fans with the latest scores and game schedules, as well as information on players, teams, and baseball history.

The Official Site of the Washington Nationals
http://washington.nationals.mlb.com/index.jsp?c_id=was
The Washington Nationals official site includes the team schedule and game results. Visitors can also find late-breaking news, biographies of Bryce Harper and other players and coaches, and much more.

Sports Illustrated Kids
http://www.sikids.com
The *Sports Illustrated Kids* website covers all sports, including baseball.

Index

Photo Acknowledgments

The images in this book are used with the permission of: © G. Fiume /Getty Images Sport/Getty Images, front cover; © Brace Hemmelgarn/Getty Images, p. 4; © The Washington Post/Getty Images, p. 5; © Brad Mangin /Stringer/Getty Images, p. 6; © Jim McIsaac/Getty Images, p. 8; © iStock /Thinkstock, p. 9; © Jim Toomey/Alamy, p. 10; Seth Poppel Yearbook Library, p. 13, 14, 15, 17; © Mark J. Rebilas/USA TODAY, p. 18, 19, 20, 21; © McClatchy-Tribune/Getty Images, p. 22; © Andrew Weber/USA TODAY, p. 23, 24; © Rob Tringali/Stringer/Getty Images, p. 25; © Brad Mills/USA TODAY, p. 26; John G. Mabanglo/Newscom, p. 27; © Dilip Vishwanat/Stringer/Getty Images, p. 28; © Mitchell Layton/Getty Images, p. 29.

Front cover:© G. Fiume/Getty Images Sport/Getty Images.

Main body text set in Caecilia LT Std 55 Roman 16/28.
Typeface provided by Adobe Systems.